Emma Lou Thayne

“The hallmark of her life—as a woman, as a writer—is balance. She seems to have a stability and steadiness that could be traced to the equilibrium of her early home life . . . she may have become the voice of her people and culture.”

Deseret News

“Emma Lou Thayne seems exultant…her sensitivity to the texture of language, her absolute harmony with nature, her unwavering faith in the human spirit…”

Marriage and Family
St. Abby Press

“…leaps all sorts of hurdles without even noticing them…to square fundamental values with reality…”

Salt Lake Tribune

“Emma Lou Thayne’s poems are honest and strong, written in images bright with mountain freshness…pulls us deep into our own rememberings. We come away knowing we have read poems that are mature and important.”

Ann Stanford

Books by Emma Lou Thayne

Spaces in the Sage

Until Another Day for Butterflies

A Woman's Place

On Slim Unaccountable Bones

Never Past the Gate, a Novel

With Love, Mother

How Much for the Earth?

As for Me and My House

Things Happen
Poems of Survival

All God's Critters Got a Place in the Choir
(with Laurel Thatcher Ulrich)

Hope and Recovery
A Mother-Daughter Story of Manic Depression and Bulimia (with Becky Thayne Markosian)

The Place of Knowing, A Spiritual Autobiography
(Audio)

EMMA LOU THAYNE

New York 2010

Digital Legend Press, 2010
Content First Published by Nishan Gray, Inc., 1977

Acknowledgements are made to *The Ensign, The New Era, Utah Holiday, Humanities Review,* and *Roanoke Review* for permission to reprint material which has previously appeared in those publications

Digital Legend Press
4700 Clover St.
Honeoye Falls, NY 14472

ISBN: 978-1-934537-67-1

www.digitalegend.com

1-877-222-1960

Printed in the United States of America

Cover Design by: Kim Blackett
Photo by: Tom Smart

We must consider the home;
it is the spring of life.

David O. McKay

To those who make my belonging.

Contents

Live Center

The Private & The Unofficial

A Relative Thing

Live Center

Live Center

Of all places I never expected to be let in, this had to be the most unlikely. But there I was, almost dead center in the delivery room – of somebody else's baby! It had been nearly fourteen years since I had been strapped into that glorious point of no return, and none of the five times that I had made the entrance as one and the exit as two had ever felt like this.

Now I stood in the green garb and stifling mask of the delivery room personnel, seeing only the eyes of my tall son-in-law across the table as we watched the birth. Between us lay Becky, chatting and smiling as if we were all at a birthday party – which, of course, we were. But it had somehow never felt like that to me those years before when ours had made their arrivals. Stunned by the ease and early joy of this new approach to birthdays, all I could think was, "What a marvelous age to have a baby in!" And, of course, "What a thing I get to be a part of!"

If it hadn't been an unbusy time at the hospital, if the good doctor had not been graciously unorthodox (I must have looked comically bereft as Becky had been wheeled out of the labor room – and as Paul had said, "Hey, you oughta come along, Grey.") I never would have been standing there when it happened. But there we were, Paul and I, looking from Becky to each other to the doctor, who suddenly proclaimed, "It's a spontaneous birth! Here it comes!"

It? It! In another second, "It" became Richard Paul, black haired, lavender, wet with arrival. In a skilled off-handedness, the doctor drew mucous from the baby's throat with a syringe and said, "Now watch. They all start out kind of blue, but once the air gets in there…" In his big hands the new little Richard began to breathe. Above the clamped cord, his chest, narrower than his head, rose and fell, rose and fell. Like the slow-motion tracing of a flower opening, he turned pink. His legs drew up. He kicked. His arms flailed and his head went back. His mouth opened to a "wa, wa" that shot through me like a sudden descent in an elevator. I could not look away. Not even at Becky who was saying, "Let me see!" and was, I'm sure, seeing just what I was. I could feel her laughing.

The doctor handed Richard to the nurse who busied him through the rituals of arrival and laid him in a small square bed under a heat lamp across the room, naked and squalling. I had followed like mercury to itself and stood there looking down on the unbelievable. Only minutes before, he was not. Now he was. There in that crib a collection of fingers and ears and knees – even toenails and eyebrows – was gathered into a life. In his head was the beginning of recognition, in his legs the starts of running. Somewhere in him streamed unimaginable inclinations and potential skills. And at the core of him, most indefinable of all, was the spirit that would make it all work, the "trailing clouds of glory" that hovered palpably around his obvious indignation at being startled out of his warm darkness.

I looked up. His father's eyes met mine across the clouds, and I knew he knew. Our masks soaked up the tears that welcomed Richard to another becoming. Behind me in the room was Becky, my first-born, and before me, Paul, who had infused her with new life. And there between us now lay Richard, getting redder and redder with kicking and crying.

"Richard, you funny little geranium," I thought, "there you are, mad as a puppy in the tub, ready to burst upon whatever's out there. Your great-grandmother Warner is in you, swinging a bat for her boys to play ball after their chores on the ranch. Your great-grandfather Richards is stitching you together with his surgeon's needle and telling you to send your brain to school. Your great-great-grandfather Erickson is persuading you to take his Swedish knowing of the land to work. And your great-grandmother Markosian is striking matches in your pores to fire in you the indomitability that led her to rediscover in America the grace lost in the slaughter of her family in Armenia.

"It's true, little Richard. 'Nobody ever died that had a family.' We're all in you – in the palms of your hands and the expansions of your heart. Take over, new boy. In no time you'll be in charge. But for now, cry it out. Let the cold world know you're here, not ready, but ready.

"And we'll wait a bit to have a hand in how you go, though you can't imagine how much I want to get hold of you – to slick you up and tender you down. But then again, maybe I have already given you, without trying, the most that I can give: a chance to try. Through your mother over there I've come to get you. Welcome to a family. And now we'll have to make it – together."

First Loss

My grandma shared her bed with me
Till she died when I was twelve.
We slept with breaths that matched.
I went to sleep every night restraining
Deliberately one extra breath in five
To let her slower time teach mine to wait.

She never knew I waited, but talked
To me of Mendon where Indians ferreted
Her isolated young-wife home for cheese and
honey,
And of Santa Barbara and eerie tides that
Drew her now for gentle months away from
snow,
And sometimes of Evangeline lost in the forest
primeval.

Grandma's batter-beating, white-gloved,
laughing
Daytime self slept somewhere else, and she
visited
Mellifluous beyond my ardent reach, always off
Before me. I followed into rhythms I knew
Were good, her chamois softness weighing me
By morning toward a cozy common center.

She died there, when I was twelve.
I was sleeping, alien, down the hall
In a harder bed, isolated form the delicate
Destruction that took its year to take her.
That night my mother barely touched my hair
And in stiff, safe mechanics twirled the customary

Corners of my pillow one by one. "Grandma's gone,"
She said. Crepuscular against the only light
Alive behind her in the hall, she somehow left.
My covers fell like lonely lead on only me.
I lay as if in children's banks of white where
After new snow we plopped to stretch and carve

Our shapes like paper dolls along a fold.
Now, lying on my back, I ran my longest arms
From hip to head, slow arcs on icy sheets,
And whispered childhood's chant to the breathless room:
"Angel, Angel, snowy Angel,
Spread your wings and fly."

Brothers

To for with by among of
you
I still am
everyone
I ever have been:

  baby on your lap, Homer,
  waving both arms for us
  inside your quizzical look
  at Grandma, lens, pinetop;

  catch for your pitch, Rick,
  twin for your figuring, commandant
  for your secondary columns
  on board or draw sheet;

  barely bigger, challenge for your
    games, Gill,
  till at fourteen your curly hair
  pushed into its own shape to make my
    combings
  partner to your measured air.

You laugh with me, big brothers,
and ring my holidays
with each other's pockets

full of faith,
    of farewells smoothed with salty kisses
        and incandescent soles for my
            departures
        and unreproachful children
            with belonging in their eyes

to for with by among of us.

The greatest insurance we can have that our children will come back is to let them go.

Home is where I get to bring all of me –
and be loved.

A Sense of Proportion

A household can be full of the ties that bind – scrapbooks, journals, traditions, blackboards with messages, and a thousand meals together. It can have faith, hope and charity, but what will finally be the saving grace in any family, must be a sense of the ridiculous, especially in ourselves.

The following is an excerpt from my novel, *Never Past the Gate*, Peregrine Smith, 1975; Book Club Selection: Christian Herald Association, Chappaqua, NY.

Mother was stacking her mending on the red sewing box by the stilt rocker. She had on her best smock and under it a city dress, so Katie knew she was ready for a not-regular day. Katie suddenly longed for a normal day, and more than anything for Mother to laugh. Mother had always laughed. Once even at a family reunion. There were so many relatives there that the reunion had to be held in the recreation hall of a ward, and the program, representative talents from all branches of the family were on the stage. Mother held out pretty well for most of it, but nearly at the end a boy began a trumpet solo of the "The Lost Chord." Katie was sitting next to Mother and could feel it begin to happen. The chord was very lost; in fact even Katie, whose musical ear was not exactly exact, was pondering where it had gone. First, she felt Mother start to jiggle. She darted a glance at her and saw her fist rolled up at her mouth, her cheeks puffing and her eyes watering. They were sitting on the solid bench that surrounded the hall, in plain sight of all the relatives. Katie tried to look somewhere safe – at the vaulted ceiling, at the rear doors, at the leaded windows across the field of heads. Nothing worked. She could hear Mother stifling snorts of air and knew that James was doing the same on the other side of her. The bench began to quiver and Katie knew the piece had better end soon – the whole program had better end. "We always disgrace ourselves," Mother had said time and again. "And it's all your fault," she'd smile, paddling one of their bottoms and starting to laugh again remembering. Sometimes they managed to make it to a safe ending, where Mother would daub her eyes and nose daintily with her lace hanky as if she had been terribly moved, and sigh back into control. But at the reunion the end failed to come soon enough. Just before the final phrases of the trumpet, Mother had burst out with what she would have labeled a most unladylike noise. The whole audience had turned to watch as Mother led the procession of her disgraced family out for a drink of water…

I Marry You

What was I?
What roused my day?
What pampered night?
What brought yellow roses hovering about
    like fairies that scampered
    from my childhood
    when the light went on
    but left their whimsy
    for my private eyes?
What is it that you bring?

What was I? What gave the salt,
    the burning clove?
    What rescued quietly abandoned dreams
    like a plankton moving
    toward the unseen motion
    of a changing moon?
Where have you taken me?

Before the bringing
and the taking,
what made me know enough
to marry you?

The Building

(To Neruda)

We built us a place.

I had built it first in childhood

in trees and underground
and brought it home draped
in sage brush and mountain flowers.

Then I built it in blue skies
and hung it with silent dispatch
on the morning and rich night.

When I grew up and the family came
and the land by the old pace,
cement, wood and glass
took over our story.
They were almost as important as time
and it was necessary to go looking.

And so the trucks began to come.

They stuttered up the steep ground
and unloaded stacks
and more stacks.

The columns dug into the hillside
and we posed on them as past beginning –
but it was nowhere near enough.
It needed cement, wood, glass, screen,
    doors –
And I was done with sleeping.

But it kept becoming.
The floors became,
and then the windows,
not windows so much as new hangings
in the clear air. Working,
pushing out and up with eye and hand,
it kept on becoming
until it was able to look out of the windows,
and it seemed that after such a stacking of
    stacks
there would be a roof that would reach up
and finally have a hand in morning
and night.

I gave myself to little else but finding what
    was needed.
To an old coal stove put out of its house
I said, "Come, warm us," and to another
    way past memory, "Cook for us."
And to abandoned seats
I offered food and a place to be seated.

To the wood I said, "Be a wall – to do
    more than
hold up the sky; you will be there for girls
to festoon with colors; you will hover
    about Nicky's nap."

That brought us to the paint
which had to be there to stay –
earth flooding wood, sunshine on beams
so that they would begin to sing,
the stairs and railings to stretch
up to finger the pines holding the corners.

Time is short. Winter is almost here.

Wood, glass, pipe,
hinges and locks must be selected.

Still, the building on the mountain keeps
    on becoming,
a pounding of pulses in its extensions,
the carpenter, knowing, hammering
and sawing the boards we will be
walking, sleeping and eating on.

Many parts of my life go without notice.

The cabin grows and is itself
in the oldest place we know.

It alone is unawed by what it says.
It stands on its own feet,
wears warm fittings over its spine
and kisses the arena of Mt. Air Canyon.

Now we can rest. This is the cabin:

For all to come, all we will need will be
          time:
what it needs now is a chance to blossom.
And that will come

under the snow

and in the spring.

Only the place that fits my dimensions
both holds and frees me.

Preface

When a mother by necessity or inclination – or both – is busy with interests away from home, it is easy to be plagued by concern over "Who or what have I neglected today?"

Regardless of the importance of what pulls her away – learning, civic or church work, enrichment – she wonders if she can make up to those at home what her absence has taken away.

Sometimes there are strange manifestations that show how one can manage to be never really out of the home – even when out of sight.

Bread May Come Back Cake

(First published in *The Ensign*, June 1971)

That Monday night was a lot like other nights with the family. We had had a time of haphazard togetherness with our five daughters and now, filled with the spirit of getting on with it, we were ready for dessert when Shelley, a fifteen-year-old sophomore in high school, snapped her fingers and lit up.

"Hey, Everybody," she said, "wait a minute. Before you go I want to read you something really neat."

She wheeled out of the room and returned in a minute waving a piece of typing paper.

"I want to read you this – I got it from my teacher last week. It's all about how not to let the group get to you – about just being yourself and relaxing and not worrying about what other people are thinking all the time."

She began to read:

"It is important that you do not become so enamored of the idea of belonging to a group that you lose focus on what you hope to be as an individual. You are truly a child of God and as such you have been given the blessing of standing erect and saying to yourself, 'I am only one, but I am one.' And even though you need and desire very much to be part of something bigger than yourself, you can carry into every group a divine right to say yes or no, to participate or to walk away. After all, the Lord's kingdom is founded upon that very right, the free agency that allows each of us to make choices.

"Plagued as we are by being all too human and all too desperate for the support of those we love, still integrity, honesty, and the beautiful peace of a clear conscience are not things to be dealt with lightly. No group is worth the sacrifice of these things. And no group is so amazingly wonderful that it cannot be replaced by another.

"Your life is a one-time thing, to be guarded, respected, and given the tender, loving care of an owner who can offer it only the choicest of settings for growth and eternal progression."

As she read, I had a vague feeling that I had heard that somewhere before. Shelley was still beaming. "Our Mutual teacher gave everyone in the class a copy."

Needled by remembering and yet not remembering, I slipped into my cubbyhole where bookcases overhang my typewriter, and began to browse through a current church manual whose pages leaped with memories. For two years I had been on a committee which had agonized in happy labor over the slow emersion of that manual. Every paragraph I read swelled with what had gone into the making of those lessons. I remembered the crises of writing them and of getting approval from what seemed a thousand places. The whole manual is about groups.

I came to page 37, right-hand column, lesson 4, called "One of Us." It began, "Tell your girls that it is important that they do not become so enamored of the idea of belonging to a group…"

When I wrote those words, I had been talking to some generic girl – a mythical fifteen-year-old that I knew I loved in the abstract, a girl whose life I wanted to touch through some teacher way off out there, a girl who might or might not listen, but a girl who mattered very much.

Tonight I heard my Shelley, my fifteen-year-old, reading my words with a reverence reserved only for awesome authority. My Shelley / my words – fused in a moment of learning that no casual or formal motherly promptings could have elicited.

When I showed her the book and the words, we both laughed. She blurted out, "Mom, come on! You didn't really write that, I thought it was Shakespeare or somebody really important."

"Yeah, Shell," I said, as I ate my cake – and had it, too.

To My Stillborn Child

We lived together,
You and I,
Fed from tables
Where I chose with
Unaccustomed caution
Wanting vibrance
On a spoon
Or strength by glass,
Certain of your
Tasting too.

Nights, I willed
My possibles to you,
Prayed whatever right
Was in me
To be yours.

Mornings, meadow larks
And yellow sun
I filtered consciously
Through layered pores
To let you
In your silent darkness
Sense your daily birthright.

Afternoons I ran us both
Beyond the edges
Sometimes pressed
By wisdom and propriety,
Extending every boundary
That jealous time imposed.

Through private months
We grew
As one.

Now, with sudden silence
We are two,
You perfect in your tiny grace
But quiet as the hush of sunset
And as beautiful in passing,
Me cavernous and so alone,
I wonder that I ever was before you.

I take your hand
So small its curling
To my finger fits like petals
To a stamen,
And you re-enter me
As love incarnate,
Private, throbbing there,
Anointing every pore
With roaring peace.

When tears have gone
(they say they will)
I'll take to making sure
That I refurbish
All the spaces left by you
With what we two fed on
With you there.

As I grow older,
So will you
Wherever you are fed
By substance that
I cannot know.

And when we touch again,
More than soul to soul,
I'll take your hand –
Or you'll take mine –

And as few others can
We two will know just what it means
To grow as one.

(Adapted from a poem first published in *The Ensign*, September 1973)

Somewhere My Children

I never get used to the absence.
I close my eyes
but some clock pecks at the dark
and a lost firefly threads his strangeness
over my covered leg.

Where are you, my children,
nebulous as night,
stirring in my crevices?

Without ages you come for me.
you reach and run
and smile on my entreaties
never staying anyone the same.

You sift the years like
cinnamon in sugar
swirling through yourselves
and tumbling onto me
until I cannot breathe
for wanting to be home.

After the Wedding

It is the slow putting back
that disarranges the calm.

At this time yesterday
the whole place ran with fixing up,
all of us courtiers to the proceedings
that precede events
like birth or death
or marriage.

Even the dog was left home.
Men came away from offices
and aunts and cousins flustered
hors d'oeuvres and practices into place.

Musicians sounded their wares
and small boys made tracks in the ice cream.

She in my dress now twenty-six years yellow
and her fit groom
stood in the splendid grass
and grew smiles
as long as they could
before he came pounding on the door
where she had gone to change her seasons.

Crashes occurred in my silence.

Goodbye hands reached for her,
and wearing his cowboy hat
he was way above anyone,
past permission,
and with their destinations written in their quick soles,
she hurried to throw her bouquet of stories
into her sisters below.

The ten-year-old almost had it.
but that would not have been right.
It takes more distance for even the nearest of kin
to snatch the pain of the innocent.

They hardly watched the flocks of words
lighting them off.

And now they have gone
all of them:
Into the wilds the pair,
back to watering lawns with fences of sand
and to vanishing into broken mirrors the others.

And in this cool place of wilting names and baby's
    breath
I am putting her slip
into the laundry bag
and eating white frosted cake
as I vacuum up the blanks
and wonder where they go.

A good marriage is an adventure in mutuality.

The most credible support I can give my family is to give them chances not to lean.

To say "Follow me" is hardly inviting if the path I take is not making me happier for my being on it.

Son-in-Law

I wondered how it would be
to have a boy. Not a single one
but many: A soft one
to swaddle in kisses
without reservation.

One of fine threads concealed
in the spareness of cowboys.
One with daring arms able
to edify the exultation
of movement.

One with a welter of impulses,
extravagant and virile
in gentle comings and goings.
One with forebearance
of the tottering world
and the tentative gestures
hoping for love.

One with audacity
but no show of bravado,
no mask of pedigree,
no weaponry except instinct,

faith and himself
for survival.

One animated by the simplest of things:
school bells, the silk of a petal,

the touch of a string, the lash of an ideal.
One to make beautiful passes
at the blazing secrets
and come up cherishing the earth.

There was no reason to improvise
what I never had.
Only to wait
in my sea of days
and the bounty of my daughters.

Some other island
fashioned this singular son,
all of it in him,
to liven like a barrage of salt
these years
trembling with passing.

Goodnight

Softly aging here
I move from bed to bed
and measure out my tired time
in lengths along their languid, covered legs.

Five daughters sleeping to my touch
spread across the pillows
honeyed to their hair –
they take my kiss in ways as different
as their eyes and ages.

Eight balls up tighter,
nudges me, and sighs.
Fifteen startles wide and then
collapses into quiet recognition,
smiling. Seventeen hardly stirs but
breathes against my cheek some
gentle sound. Twelve tenses, turns,
and pulls me down in fierce acknowledgment.
And nineteen rolls away and covers up my
brazen tattoo on her cheek.

I move toward the stairs
Vulnerable, divided into fifths,
and come to you
to be made whole.

(First published in *The Ensign*, May 1971)

It is a blessed child who is loved for difference as much as for sameness.

I function best as a mother of children when I am most aware of being a child of God.

It is the quality, not quantity, of presence in a home that makes all the difference.

The Private &
The Unofficial

The Private and the Unofficial

"Family" –
It is meals, bedtime, socks and tonsils.
It is bills, deadlines, a piano and tennis shoes.
It is a high chair, a bike, a formal, a veil.

It's *Give Said the Little Stream*, Mozart and John
Denver.
It's a test in math and a game of checkers,
a soggy pillow and a fast cuckoo clock.

It's the only thing never lost in the wash,
one thing never found in a bottle or prescription.
It multiplies by division and adds as it subtracts.

It can be cold or hot, and one condition can feed
the other.

It is more than the sum of its parts:
It is an amalgam that makes each of its components
bigger –
or smaller – than when alone.

It can feed or drain, restore or devastate
because it is the working of the workings.

It deals in the private and the unofficial.

Only it can know itself – and then only sometimes.
Since it is a resource upon which all other resources
        draw,
        it must be observed and nurtured as nothing else.

It needs attention and care
    so that it can be attentive and caring.

And like prayer, what flows around and within it
    is the great nourisher… .

Verse from a Nine Year Old

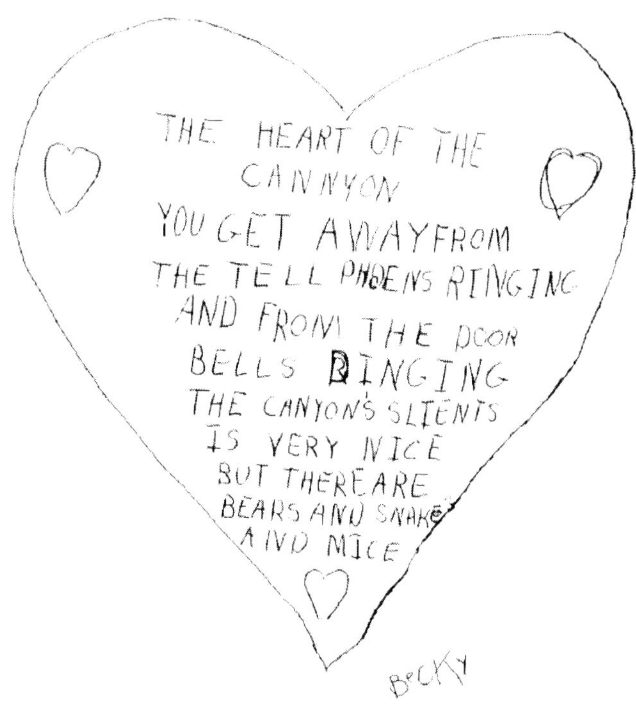

Notes on two sides of a laundry cardboard written by my long-married

Dearie—
Hate to go
without you
Please remember
your pills and
call me as soon
as you get to office.
Glass of milk poured
in refridge
Love
"G"

Mother and Father two weeks before his fatal stroke.

"FLOSSIE" —
YOU CUTE LITTLE
CUSS! I AM SITTING
HERE WAITING FOR "TIME"
FOR PILLS NOT TO
REACT UNFAVORABLY. JUST
FAVORABLY AS HOMER WANTS
THEM TO.
HAD EVERYTHING. (TO EAT)
READ EVERYTHING.
ENJOYED EVERYTHING
BUT YOU. THIS OLD
CASTLE IS GREAT. BUT
VACANT, SO VACANT, WITHOUT
YOU IN IT.
I DO LOVE YOU
"PUG"

From a talk given by a daughter

By Rinda, age 20

I guess one of the things I remember most about Dad in my childhood days was his whistle. Every day as soon as lunch was over we'd start looking forward to the time when Dad would come home, and at 6:00 we'd hear the door open and Dad do his special whistle and come in to set down his briefcase, take off his coat, and play with us. He'd swing us around, and help us stand on our heads and let us climb all over him. Or he'd be the horse and see how many of us could stack up on top of him at once. It was Dad that would give me the grizzly bear hug every night and scratch me with his whiskers and tell me about the seals he saw with Aunt JoAnn and the little boy who stuck his finger in the dike. It was Dad that would sing the Lord's Prayer and turn red and feel bad when I'd burst out laughing. And it was always Dad who would take me for a hike even if he was tired, or let me keep a kitten even though he hated cats, and it was Dad who took me to sprees to Ogden to see Nana and who dried my tears and let me be his little girl. To me, my Dad could do no wrong. He was the strongest man, the best skier, the smartest person…and certainly the most trusted.

When I think back on my earlier years with Dad, one night stands out in my mind. It was a night just before Christmas and we were all gathered in the living room watching TV. This show was the saddest show you could ever imagine, but especially for us because we'd always had a hard time sitting through Lassie without crying. But this show was especially sad and we were all watching the ending as this little boy had to give away all his little brothers and sisters because both of his parents had been killed, and we all had big lumps in our throats and were trying so hard not to be the first to burst out crying, when all of a sudden we heard this big sob from Dad's chair and saw him sitting there bawling his eyes out. Well, soon after we all joined in and started hugging each other and saying how glad we were that we didn't have to give each other away. And then we went to bed. But that night stayed with me for a long tine, because I'd realized that Dad could cry; and since then one of the things I have come to love the most about him is that he is a man that can cry; a man that never lets pride or vanity stand in his way. He can be telling us about his old friends in Brigham, or the summer he met Mom, or anything that is deeply meaningful to him, and cry like a baby. And somehow I have come to respect and love him because he is able to feel deeply and express it openly.

Dad never ceases to be patient and gentle and kind, with the kind of patience only a father can have. He and Mom have somehow exposed us to all the good things in life, and for this we are indeed grateful. Dad has taught us the satisfaction that comes from working hard and being honest and trustworthy. We have learned the principles of the gospel and of life, and the joy that comes from sharing spiritual as well as physical and emotional experiences. Mom and Dad have shown us the sunshine, the new snow, the smooth lakes, the mountains... the excitement of every-day living, and have also encouraged us to try new paths of our own. But through all the learning and testing and discovering we have had each other and Dad as our foundation. I guess as I grew up I began to know Dad as a man, not just as a father. I think it took me till junior high to realize he wasn't the world's greatest skier; in fact, he never has gotten out of his snowplow. And I found he couldn't figure out my algebra and that he had doubts and fears of his own. Yet somehow, though we have expanded and changed considerably through the years, we still listen for the door to open and hear Dad's whistle. We still find the same security in his now annoying bear hugs, and we still find ourselves wanting to be his little girls, because he has provided us with a quiet love and faith and strength that defy time and change.

Two approaches of a little girl to managing her parents

Dear Mom,

Tonight I read
the first chapter of
the Wonderful flight
to the illushrroom planet,
and I've practiced, and
I got meg to bed. So
please let me sleep at
Cindy's house tommoro
please, Please, if you
like the note I wrote
you yesturday
I hope you like this
better! Please if I'm
back by 10:30 Please.
I
ever
hemed
my
dress Please, Please, Please

Roses are red
Voliets are blue
I'll do my reading
So can I sleep too?!

Love your
daughter Dinny

Because she was blonde with dark-haired sisters she imagined she was adopted

Dear [redacted] Mom, Your adapted child has ran away. I ran to some place where people will love me and take care of me. Not people who will ground me and no one else. Not people who want me to leave. Not people who don't give you any dinner when you ur starving and really don't want you to live. Not people who will make you go to bed at the same time your 6 year old sister does. The people who do do these things are my family. Mom I did A boo-boo at the top I was suposto put Dear Step mom, because I'm adapted. Is that what you call people mothers, when they adoptad? Well! anyway I hate you has much as you hate me, but you hate me more. I won't ever be coming back so I better say good-bye for the last time.

Good-bye

[redacted] hate, your adapted one Denny.

P.S. Do you hate me as much as I think you do?

Letter from a newly-married daughter

PAUL AND I FINALLY PUT THE BOOKS AWAY AND IMMEDIATLY FELL ASLEEP. I WOKE UP HOURS LATER ONLY TO VIEW THE MOST SPLENDID SIGHT IN THE WORLD! THE FULL MOON WAS JUST ABOVE CASTLE CRAGS AND I WAS ABSOLUTELY AWED AT THE SILENT, SPARKLING SILENCE. EVERYTHING OUTSIDE WAS AGLOW - TALK ABOUT AN ENCHANTED FOREST - OH, HOW YOU WOULD HAVE LOVED IT, MOTHER. WHY AREN'T YOU HERE? WHAT B.Y.U. CONFERENCE, WHAT OBLIGATIONS AND COMMITMENTS ARE MORE IMPORTANT THAN THIS? ONCE AGAIN I LAY BACK AND LET MY MIND WANDER BACK TO DAYS AND NIGHTS IN THE CANYON AS A LITTLE GIRL. MUD PIES AND MOSS VILLAGES, HUTS AND HIKES, CANYON BREAKFASTS, CANYON TOAST, CANYON ANYTHING AND EVERYTHING - HOW MARVELOUS! HOW VITALLY IMPORTANT! FROM THE CRIB IN THE OLD CABIN, TO THE FOLD-OUT BED ON THE PORCH, TO [illegible]'S BED AND THE GUEST BED, THE "ROCKY MOUNTAIN" AND "THE BOARD," FROM EACH OF THOSE OLD BEDS I BROUGHT MY DREAMS TO THIS NEW PLACE.

JUST LET ME THANK YOU FOR LETTING PAUL AND ME LOVE THIS PLACE AS YOU DO . . . FOR LETTING ME BE A PART OF THE PLANNING AND THE DOING AND THE DREAMING AND MOSTLY OF THE KNOWING THAT I CAN PASS THIS SAME "CANYON SPIRIT" ON TO MY CHILDREN AND MY CHILDREN'S CHILDREN AND ON AND THAT IT WILL BE A FOREVER, ETERNAL FEELING.

I LOVE YOU,

SHELLEY

Poem from a youngest sister

Why Cant I Hold This Rainbow

I set my fork down
Surprised at my small appetite.
Mom and Dad talked of an
upcoming wedding and wondered if
they would have time to make it.
I ~~sighed~~ took a deep breath, impatient at thier talk,
~~and~~ my hectic day
settled thick and grey in my head
and blurred my eyes and made my
aching bones heavy in my chair.
I looked at the other end of the table
at four vacant seats.
It was like a pallet with ~~all~~ only a few colors left.
Lets see,
that chair would be green
Becky would be green.
Green like her bathrobe ~~or~~ with her
brown hair scattered over her sholder
like a pine tree against the brown earth.
The green would ~~vary~~ change in shade
~~but~~ and with each variation, I would
paint with awe.
She laughed such a good laugh,
and her constant caring often brought
my brush back to green.
That chair would be blue.
yes Rinda is a light blue.
I used to brush Rindas long hair
while she told me stories of her
childhood and her many kittens.
I would paint Rinda with delacacy

and ~~hope tha~~ the soft blue
would bring out her genteelness and
her understanding,
which would cause me to only dab on
the blue conservatively,
because of my need for it.
That chair would be yellow.
Shelley is definitely yellow.
Yellow like the sun that gave freely
of itself to ~~Shelley~~ her.
Yellow like a lemon - tangy ~~and~~ that livens
the tastebuds.
~~yellow made~~ Painting with yellow was
always easy, and I applied it boldly.
And there would be Dinny.
Pink.
Pink like a rose bud
or pink like her cheeks before a date
which tears would easily stream
down at a sad movie.
Or pink like her parka
which made her unique
and her color cherishable.

But now the chairs ~~were colorless~~ are empty,
except for Dinnys coming and going.
And the individual colors have been
deluted with new hues, and washed
off my pallet.
They have left me here,
with cloudy eyes,
hoping for a rainbow.

Megan

Letter from a new son-in law

and families, blessed families--
I am back from the underworld,
I am Joseph out of the pit--
thank you for bringing me to
this sweet hour, for showing
me that despite all loss, frustra-
tion and trouble, things do
work out... in the old cabin,
among the great, green mountains, this heritage of
strength, goodness and love
is now mine too. Thank you
for this -- to you I sing--
"Blessed be the tie
that binds our hearts..."

Your new son,

A daughter, about her Grandmother

By Dinny, age 14

One experience that probably brought us closer together than any other happened just before Christmas and it involved our bigger family – cousins, aunts and uncles – and most of all our Father in Heaven.

For fifteen years our grandmother, Grace Richards Warner, lived with us. When my older sister Becky was a baby my grandmother tried to teach her to say "grandmother," but all she could get out was "grandmu…t." So always after she was known as "Mut," not only to the family but also to almost anyone who came to see us. It was ironic that everyone called her this because she was so dignified that she called even our dearest next-door neighbors and friends "Mr. and Mrs." She would never have admitted it, but I think she liked the affection that went with the name.

I remember the day (I think I was 12) when I realized I was taller than Mut. It really made me feel big and grown up, but as I grew older I realized I really wasn't that tall – it was just that she was only 4'10". She always wore her hair in a bun unless she had just gotten back from the hairdresser; then it would be ringlets, which she'd laugh about and try to get combed before she got caught. She had a car of her own and a lot of times it scared people for her to drive down the street because they didn't think anyone was at the wheel. She was so small she could barely see over the dashboard.

No one had more idiosyncrasies than Mut. She'd always ask one of my sisters or Mother or Dad to drive her "up the hill." That was up the block so she could "sprint home to help her middle." And on her walk she couldn't forget her hat, gloves, her shoe bag, and walking shoes, no matter how hot the weather. No lady would ever leave the house without them! Speaking of weather, every time one of her children or grandchildren was on a trip, no one had to worry much, for Mut, who had more faith than anyone I've ever knew, was with absolute confidence "working on the weather."

Mut loved beauty in design, in character, in language and in life. She gave it away every chance she got, to all of us and to literally hundreds of friends and acquaintances whose needs she always found time to be interested in. On the Sunday before last Thanksgiving, when Dad was away at a convention, Mut drove the rest of us all to dinner for a spree. On Monday she was taken to the hospital with a severe heart attack. She was in intensive care for 5 days, where only her children could visit, and on Friday she went into a coma. After she had been in a coma for 9 hours, not responding to anything, the doctors decided to move her to a private room so all the rest of us could see her, maybe for the last time. At this point my Uncle Homer, who was one of her doctors, told all of us that the chance of her surviving with all her faculties was about 0. All of the family – about 35 of us – gathered in her room at the hospital. My mother, who was her only daughter, could not stand to see Mut just drift away – it wasn't like her to go without a real try. This wasn't Mut. She didn't give up. Mother squeezed her hand, swollen from needle punctures, and spoke into her ear, "Come on, Mother…you can do it…Come on!"

And then Mom said, "She squeezed back!" That room was filled with all of her loved ones and with a spirit I'll never forget. We were all in touch with the biggest force in anybody's life – love and faith and a belief in what those things can do. We were crowded around her bed, all crying and sending our deepest love to that dear little lady and our most urgent prayers to our Father in Heaven. Meg was standing even with

Mut's head, and we all watched as very slowly Mut opened her eyes and looked straight into Meg's. For a minute they just looked and then Mut barely smiled. For hours she had not responded to anything, and now we knew she knew we were there and loving her. Mother said, "Mother, here's Shelley," and unbelievably Mut began to turn over, with her other little swollen hand reaching for Shelley's. Then Mom said, "Mother, here's Dinny," and I slowly moved towards her. Both soft little arms came reaching up and pulled me down to her.

I can't tell you how I felt. I had been part of a miracle! The doctors couldn't believe that she was conscious, but later that night on our way home, Becky, Megan and I went in and told her goodnight and with her brown eyes open, she slowly whispered her first words – "Good night."

By 2:00 that morning, my Uncle Homer was bending over her to try to get her to sip some broth, and as he leaned down in his lab coat, she said to her grown-up son, "You're missing a button!" Then we knew she was back – alert, funny, concerned. This was our Mut.

Still, although she remained bright and never complained, her attack had been so massive that it was just a question of time until her lungs would fill up with fluid and she would die. But she never let on that she knew – and neither did we. After two weeks in the hospital with all of us there every day, the doctors decided to let her come home where she loved to be and where we could take care of her. I'll never forget those two and a half weeks when we had the privilege of talking with her and watching Dad and Mom and the other adults in the family face the fact of death with serenity. No one talked about it; everyone just lived quietly the belief that this was surely not any real end.

Saturday night, the night before Christmas Eve, I had had a good talk with Mut but I was afraid she felt she wouldn't make it to the holiday that she loved most of all. Every year for Christmas she had a clothesline strung in the living room and hung on it an outfit for each one of her children and grandchildren. This Christmas she'd sent all of us shopping for each other, to be sure the clothesline would be ready. But that night, with my mother and dad and all my uncles and aunts there, she had been looking at some new flowers just sent to her, when suddenly she took a big gasp and was gone.

I never felt sadder in my life, and yet I couldn't help feeling kind of happy too, thinking of the Christmas she'd be having with Grandpa. And our Christmas was really special, too. Our family – the cousins and all – have always been close and have had a lot of fun together, but it's easy to take for granted how blessed we are with having people to love. On that Christmas day we had the clothesline and everyone got a gift from Mut – clothes, yes – but far more. We all got a new feeling for each other and for the real meaning of Christmas, The fact that we'd all someday be together just as surely as we were that day. I've never been more thankful or felt so blessed, thanks to a cute little lady that brought so much into my life and the lives of everyone she came in contact with.

A Relative Thing

Blend

I'm part of you, you're part of me –
That's what's called my "family."

Somewhere housed behind a door,
between a ceiling and floor,
are people who not only care
what food I eat and what I wear,
but more than this, are first to see –
and share with me discovery!

This world is wide, and living blooms
with promise far beyond our rooms.
So run with me to look, to find -
or if you will, just wait behind,
being what you best can be –
caring for the "me" in me.

And in my travels, pulse and pore
will tell me I am something more
than just unique and on my own –
you'll be there too, not me alone.
For you're my immortality,
My larger self, my family.

(First published in Mia Maid Manual, Discovery, The Church of Jesus Christ of Latter-day Saints, 1967-68)

Trust is the healthiest by-product
of a happy home

Lucky are the children who are taught that to
praise one is not to condemn another.

The sure sign of a big person is his ability to
delight in the success of others.

Late Waiting

It's good they know about fire,
    how to build one
    by laying kindling across the paper
    rolled and wrung
    in the base of the stove or pit:

    how to put on
    coal, large or small, to fit
    the burning time;

    how to control the smoke and size
    of the flame
    by adding
    fuel or damping;

    how to temper
    its end
    with caustic
    or time;

    the caution to give to
    smoldering;
    how to throw out ashes.

They've known since they were children
    begging to strike
    the match.

There's no tending now the fires
    they build
    and light.

    Only the hope that they know
    how and when and whether
    to stir
    to keep the fire
    in its place.

Obedience given without respect
    corrupts the gentlest soul.

A Family Is More than a Relative Thing

You do not live with us.

That is, you do not occupy
this house.

But you belong –
in some ways more than any who go daily
in and out that door.

Like April, your arrival,
even when expected, is surprise,
fresh and full of promise
as a violet in bud.

And your stay is precious
for its passing,
your sure connections fused
by more than just capricious blood.

Ninety-Five

Welcome to my attic.
It's small and crowded
But where I spend me.
No one comes
At least not now.
Why should they?
No one knows my name.
Oh, certainly, that -
Aunt Kate, Miss Stayner.
But not my name.

No one knows a thing.
Who ever saw me dance
    or ride the pinto at the fair
    or snitch Brother Brewer's cherries
    or catch the street car
    or drive an auto before the mayor could
    or buy a radio that got New York
    or sell twenty-seven ads one month
    or hear Myrt and Marge at 9 five nights
        a week
    or be a missionary in Detroit
    or sing for Rueben – high C – even him
        surprised

or make a flowered hat
or get some land to give away
or see Alaska
or watch his buggy disappear behind
the dust?

See my boxes full of boxes.
Open them enough
And here I am:
Too far away for anyone
To call me Katherine.

The best insurance I bring to the longevity of a relationship is the ability to deal wholesomely with change.

Three Profound Rules for Oblique Housekeeping

or

How to Stay on Top without seeming to Paddle

1. Never leave a room empty-handed – clutter in motion has at least a chance of finding its place.

2. Never do only one simple thing at a time.

3. Never underestimate the power of fifteen minutes.

What respect do I show for eternity if I do not relish today?

Coming Home

Don't move a chair,
Don't change a picture!
Keep the tastes and smells the same.
Fix a meal, and I'll be there
Knowing every niche by name.

Bring out scrapbooks,
Play old music,
Be prepared to reminisce.
Hold to sounds, cling to looks
That I could never stand to miss.

Don't write unless
It's all unaltered,
Keep the changes secret, please.
Honor keepsakes. I confess
I'm counting on my memories.

So call them all!
We'll raise the table
Laughing at familiar jokes.
Hold our places, large or small,
I'm coming home to find my folks.

How Far is Down, Father?

Today I went to that mountain,
the one we climbed every Fourth of July.
It's not that steep
But then I didn't run.

Was I five the first time?
Your khakis sandpapering my wrist
below our hands, your Bunyan boots
cutting the sharp white-rock path to crescents,
you pacing me groundless to the ridge.

Our seats, the red cliffs sanded into hollows,
Sego lilies spidering the cleft, purple sky and
stomach-grabbing fear that rattlers might undo
themselves along the cracks. Milk-warm oranges.
Smashed tuna sandwiches. Melted Hersheys. A stone
thrown out to see how far down was.

One year you let me wait high on the Devil's
Slide, you jarring down ahead, shoulders heaving
in your shirt, soles showing. You turned and waved,
expecting me.

I started down like you easy, bouncy.
But down was farther than I thought
and steeper. Frantic legs
jack hammering. Windmill arms. Jammed face.

Slope sucking me. Eyes aching open,
then – crushed closed. I sprawled in dumb surrender.

But you surrounded me. Sudden, fierce,
your chest against my fall, safe
among white rocks and pines.

Today I came down slow, feeling for footholds,
clutching at my woman's urge to run here to
your grave.

(First published in *The New Era*, November 1975)

It is through my own father that I am made most able to account for a Father in Heaven.

What presumption for me to strive for godliness with so little notion of how to handle being human.

The Getting There

In the beginning alone there was a splendid kind of thrill to that late afternoon, the kind that you feel somehow may have been reserved for only the young. There was the festive excitement of a tournament, probably not too different from the exhilaration in the court of King Arthur when the jousting was about to begin. There was a crowd, milling about in their expectations. There was somewhere the succulence of holiday food prepared for contestants and spectators. Officials scurried their importance around, excitement rustled like drapery, and the time was at hand.

No doubt the improbability of my being there was the biggest factor in the strange euphoria that overcame me as I warmed up for what was to be that day an amazing recapitulation of so many of the best parts of my life. It was the semi-final round of the National Senior Indoor Tennis Championships, and I, a fifty-two-year-old wife, Relief Society teacher, mother of five, grandmother of two and three quarters, grey-haired sitter at a typewriter, was out there trying to hit the ball in ways that would not make my skilled partner ashamed of me. And across from us were the Number One team in the nation –

also sagging here and there with humid wrinkles tracing their years of playing the game and getting their ranking in the "over 50's."

A major difference had to be that it had been lots of years – decades – since I had played in a real tournament. And the reality of my doing it now suddenly mounted in my throat. What in the wild world did I think I was doing there? What made me ever think that I could waltz onto the court with the likes of these and do anything but disgrace myself and my fine partner? The four matches I'd had to play the day before now took hold of my spine and the backs of my legs. Why had it become anything but a joke to enter a tournament at all? Anything more than a pleasant chance to play in a first round and meet some interesting strangers on the court? I served three double faults in the first game. In the next I missed more service returns than I had in all four matches the day before. My eyesight failed me, my will jellied from my scalp and solidified in my immovable soles.

I glanced furtively toward the sidelines. Sitting as close as they could to the court were my big dark haired sons-in law and my big still unbalding husband, all grinning, and behind them in the more comfortable chairs were five daughters, whose matches I had watched and been part of for nearly twenty years. They all saw that I was looking, sheepish and petrified. And they each looked back in ways as private and knowing as silent touch. One clenched his fist and drew it up in a sportsman's signal of encouragement, another nodded her firm assurance, another just shook her head and beamed. They all somehow lent themselves and their lilt to my wilting. They became for me what I had always wanted us to be for each other – steadfast support in even the most unlikely endeavor. I never felt more with my crazy family. There was a blending of something I didn't quite understand. But I liked it.

I walked around the net post and bounced the yellow ball with my racket on my way to the baseline. And a funny thing. In that short walk, everything leaped into altered focus. I was a girl again, a twenty-year-old playing doubles with my brother or my best friend. The sun was shining with summer heat, my arms and legs were firm and brown, and running was the final joy. The sweet tension of tournament stretching snatched at me and released every hormone and nerve. Concentration fell around me like an animate coma. The game was on!

For the next nearly two hours I moved in a tight bliss of having combined for me what I never could have imagined possible. Yes, I was that girl again, heady with exhilaration that I would surely have supposed to be only for the young competing for their place; and I was at the same time a mature woman with new parts of me spangling on the sidelines, rooting for me – as my mother and father and brothers had done all those years ago. How I loved them in their obvious loving me in what was that moment so unexpectedly important. Here were the mystic connections, the verities that the very wise propound and the very lucky partake of.

How the match came out mattered only as a glowing surface on a deep pattern. Having them part of my trying, being the best I knew how, giving everything I had to a momentary, demanding, soaring effort, I crossed all boundaries of time and expectation.

I was carried transcendent, into a new kind of knowing: there is richness in continuity, a magnetism between stages and generations, and a rounding out of edges. On that green court that afternoon, with a partner of my same vintage and persuasions, I glimpsed the luminous threads between kingdoms.

That the match ebbed and flowed, that we went into a tiebreaker in the third set, that we almost did the whole thing, should be treat enough to remember; but that it was so much more will last me a long time. It just may stay as one of the real recognitions that only now and then is allowed us – to see the gratuities of eternity. On the court, in the heart, in the plan, the growing not old but older is probably the only way of knowing how much right there is in the journey.

About the Author

Emma Lou Warner Thayne grew up with her three brothers on horses, lakes, ski slopes, and tennis courts. A former college poetry instructor and coach of the University of Utah Women's Tennis Team, she was ranked #3 nationally in the 50-and-over doubles. Her articles, short stories and poems have won numerous distinctions and have been widely anthologized. A few of her many honors include: David O. MacKay humanities award from Brigham Young University; Honorary Doctorate and Distinguished Alumna, University of Utah; The Thayne Center for Service and Learning at Salt Lake Community College bears her name; writing and poetry awards from The Association for Mormon Letters; The Governors Commission for Women and Families: Utah Woman of Achievement Award in Recognition of a Lifetime of Contribution and Service; Cathedral of Madeleine Award for distinguished Service to the Arts and humanities.